M000078104

With a little help
from our friends...

let the journey begin...

With a little help from our friends...

by Heidi Wozniak

**Andrews McMeel
Publishing**

an Andrews McMeel Universal company
Kansas City

www.andrewsmcmeel.com
www.heidiwozniak.com

01 02 03 04 05 LPP 10 9 8 7 6 5 4 3 2 1

Library of Congress Catalog Card Number: 00-109262
ISBN: 0-7407-1616-6

ATTENTION: SCHOOLS AND BUSINESSES Andrews McMeel books
are available at quantity discounts with bulk purchase for education,
business, or sales promotional use. For information, please write to:
Special Sales Department, Andrews McMeel Publishing,
4520 Main Street, Kansas City, Missouri 64111

This little book is dedicated to
all my friends for their help along the way...especially

to Kirsten, my loyal-first and forever-best girlfriend
(may Meg and Grace be so lucky!)

and

to Bob, my loyal-last and forever-best boyfriend
(I am so lucky!)

I love you.

We made every day an
ADVENTURE!

We turned minutes into
H O U R S .

We
weathered
many storms.

We discovered our
TALENTS.

We grew in
STRENGTH
&
confidence.

We discussed life's
BIG EVENTS!

We CELEBRATED
the seasons!

We ventured into
capitalism.

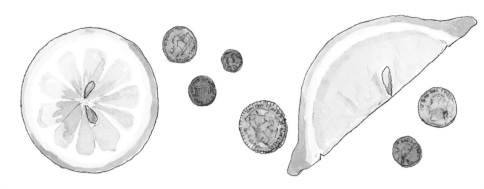

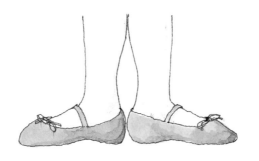

We developed
poise, grace,
and humility.

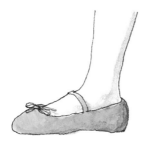 

he loves me...

he loves me not...

he loves me not...

We made BOLD
predictions.

he loves me...

he loves me...

We rejoiced our
milestones.

We SHOPPED!

We survived countless surprises!

We figured out
who we
wanted to be.

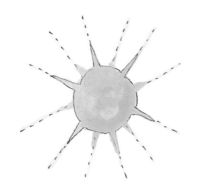

We enjoyed our day
in the SUN!

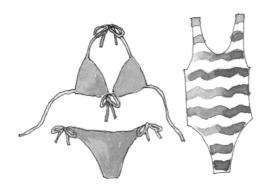

We traded traditions.

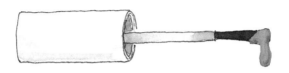

We shared secrets
and gained TRUST.

We realized
the BEST gift
is a TRUE friend.

We BRAVED the
unknown.

We dreamed of
possibilities.

With a little help from our friends

we grew up . . . TOGETHER!

and the journey continues...